Found
Moments,
Conceived
Images

*Photography from
Aurora Photos*

AURORA
PHOTOS

AURORA PHOTOS
20-36 Danforth St., #216
Portland, Maine 04101
207.828.8787
auroraphotos.com

Printed in Hong Kong
by Alcove Books.
alcovebooks.net

INTRODUCTION

Since its inception, Aurora has created and fostered strong relationships with great photographers. Over the years, our contributors have become an extended family, and these bonds, combined with the organic growth of our photographic library, have provided us with the energy to continue as a small company in a changing and very challenging marketplace. Through both calm and turbulent times, the photographers remain. Whether they are new contributors or veterans, this book reflects their spirit. It is about moments, colors and concepts, and about each photographer's contribution, reaction and interaction with the world around them.

Like a good exhibition, the images that make up this publication express a vision that comes from many sources: from the photographers themselves, with their individual styles and backgrounds; from the editors that have added their own filters as the work has come to Aurora; and of course, my own, as I pulled together images and edited the work with this book in mind.

True to our strengths, this book contains images of the outdoor world, adventure and geography. It explores cultures and social documentary. Portraiture plays a central element and transcends boundaries. Finally, and especially important to me, we've included those artistic images that simply defy classification. A commercial chord might resound through some of the work, while other images might never be licensed. In all cases, the photography is superb.

José Azel
Portland, Maine

ABOUT AURORA PHOTOS

In 1993, Aurora was founded to represent four National Geographic Magazine photographers. The company has been in business for 14 years and in that time has grown to a roster of more than 200 contributors and an assignment division, Aurora Select, in New York City.

Historically, Aurora has been an editorial stock agency with an archive of photography that has come mainly from assignments done for magazines. While many photojournalists and other magazine photographers remain at the core of the agency, our ranks are increasingly made up of stock shooters. Regardless of the source, Aurora has always enjoyed a reputation of the highest standards in single image quality, photojournalism and photographic feature stories.

Despite diminishing editorial usage fees and the challenges from bigger companies as they take on more market share, Aurora has managed to grow. One of the major turning points of Aurora's evolution came in 1995 when Aurora launched The Outdoor Collection, a mix of hardcore adventure images with lifestyle concepts to create an unparalleled library that reflects our outdoor world. The best 100 outdoor photographers in the world have joined the collection and are active contributors. It has quickly become the premier archive for outdoor photography worldwide. This collection and Aurora's ability to make gains on the commercial side of the business has put the company on a solid track. We identify our strengths as travel, geography and cultures and photojournalism, as well as the outdoors, but our true strength is simply great images that transcend cataloging.

http://www.auroraphotos.com

Woods Wheatcroft

A hiker jumps across a small pond in the Valhalla Range, British Columbia

Olivier Renck

Coke Whitworth

A Christmas tree farm in
Zionville, North Carolina

Woods Wheatcroft

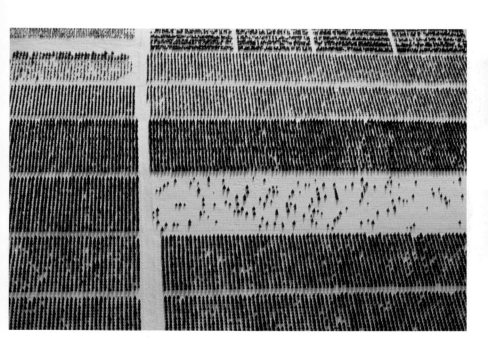

Corey Hendrickson

A beach boardwalk cuts through the sand
dunes at sunrise, Newbury, Massachusetts

David H. Wells

Desert framed by a brick
passage, Winslow, Arizona

Robb Kendrick

Randall Levensaler

Kyle George

The view downstream from Eminence Break Trail in Grand Canyon National Park, Arizona

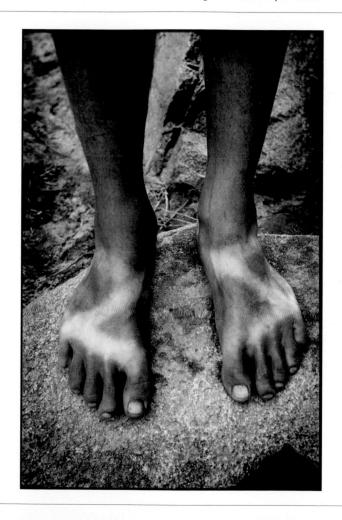

Per-Andre Hoffmann

Tungurahua volcano
eruption, Ecuador

Justin Bailie

Justin Bailie

Alexandra Daley-Clark

Hiking shoe worn through,
Appalachian Trail

Todd Korol

A gentleman strolls with his umbrella
near Piccadilly Circus in London, England

Dawn Kish

Todd Korol

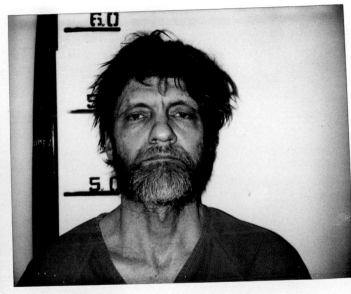

Theodore Kaczynski's mug shot taken when he was arrested

Dawn Kish

Lynn Johnson

A woman undergoes a Panchakarma massage treatment, New York City

Holly Wilmeth

Todd Bigelow

Kevin Horan

Ilja Herb

A dead, spawned chum salmon decomposes at the end of its life cycle, Goldstream, British Columbia

Shoshannah White

Ralph Talmont

Carl D. Walsh

A loon dances on the water of
Lake Tarlton, New Hampshire

Cary Anderson

Jonathan Kingston

Jen Judge

Christopher Herwig

Andrew Querner

Ron Koeberer

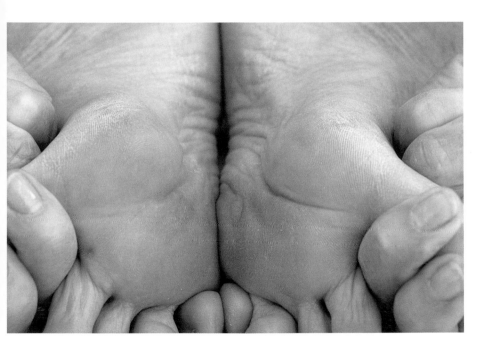

Jeff Singer

Michael Winokur

A nomadic family sleeps during the heat of the day in the desert near Timbuktu, Mali

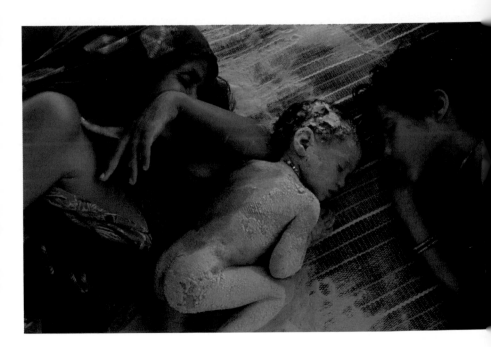

Anders Ryman

A penis sheath made of hornbill beak,
Irian Jaya, Indonesian New Guinea

Paula Lerner

Children have an intense discussion a[t]
a child care center, Kabul, Afghanista[n]

Holly Wilmeth

Michael Eudenbach

The Gibbs Hill Lighthouse
during a storm, Bermuda

Gabriela Hasbun

Beth Wald

David McLain

Andrew Kornylak

J.C. Leacock

A hiker crosses snow-covered sand dunes,
Great Sand Dunes National Park, Colorado

Chris OConnell

Paolo Marchesi

Brent Bowman and Ed Zya
fishing off the coast of Florida

Rhea Anna

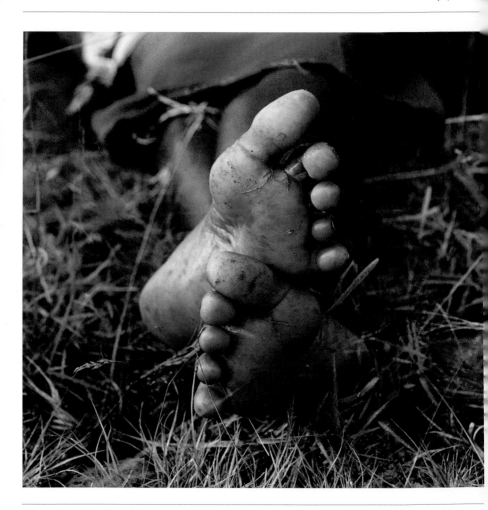

Ralph Talmont

Cary Wolinsky

Cary Wolinsky

A meditating Buddhist teacher wears sensors for making electroencephalographs

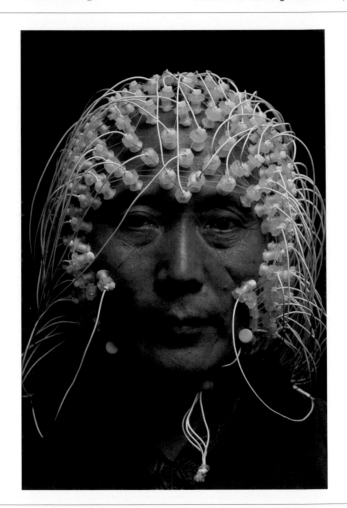

Lisa Seaman

A teenager gets his hair highlighted in a
beauty salon, San Qierico d' Orca, Italy

Gabe Palacio

Andrew Councill

Bridget Besaw

A wilderness guide transports his guests by
poling down the St. John River in Northern Maine

Melissa Farlow

Susie Post Rust

Two Bruderhof boys explore
the Pennsylvania outdoors

Bob Croslin

Alison Langley

Nick Lambert

Leaf of the colocasia
esculenta plant

megan S. Wyeth

Trees, The Netherlands
(Polaroid transfer)

David Clifford

Rebecca Roseberry laughs while
taking a break from climbing, Moab, Utah

Lars Schneider

David Stubbs

Craig Tuttle

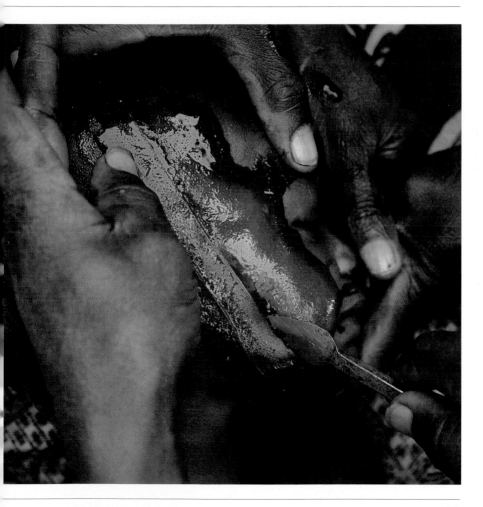

Paul Giamou

Laurie Swope

Gale Zucker

Dennis Drenner

Jay Reilly

Survivor of a village massacre,
Medellin, Colombia

Coke Whitworth

A 1947 Chevy Fleetmaster after a light dusting of snow, Vilas, North Carolina

Todd Glaser

Lars Schneider

A man stands on the roof of his campe
van overlooking canola fields in Denmar

Lars Howlett

Katja Heinemann

Campers play at Camp Heartland for children affected by HIV/AIDS, Willow River, Minnesota

Jan Sonnenmair

Children searching for salamanders,
Portland, Oregon

Ashley Gilbertson

A U.S. Marine slides down the marble
banister in Saddam's palace, Tikrit, Iraq

Andrew Cutraro

U.S. Marines move an Iraqi prisoner
at a detention center in Western Iraq

David Stubbs

Vice President Dick Cheney waves to a crowd of supporters, Jackson Hole, Wyoming

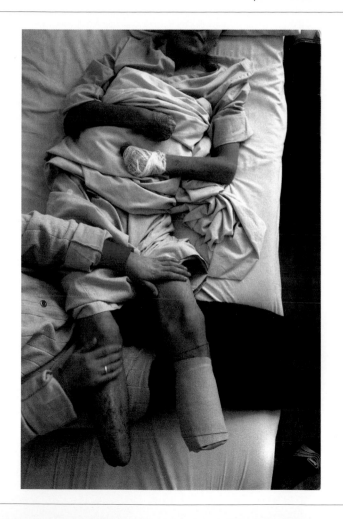

Robert Caputo

Jim Lo Scalzo

Peter McBride

Christian Heeb

Harrison Shull

A bridge crosses the fog-filled New River Gorge north of Fayetteville, West Virginia

Jake Norton

Sherpas climb in deep snow and strong winds on Gurla Mandhata, Tibet

Scott Markewitz

Bill Stevenson

Ty Milford

Henry Georgi

An ice climber solo climbs the ice at
Montmorency Falls near Quebec City

Cliff Leight

Joel Sheagren

Tom Montgomery

Dan Rafla

Simon O'Dwyer

Tom Hopkins

Scott Markewitz

Richie Schley bikes down a steep trail in Whistler, British Columbia

Patrik Lindqvist

Gabe Rogel

Aurelien Routens,
La Grave, France

Tyler Stableford

An ice climber explores a rare ice cave
inside the Langjokull Glacier, Iceland

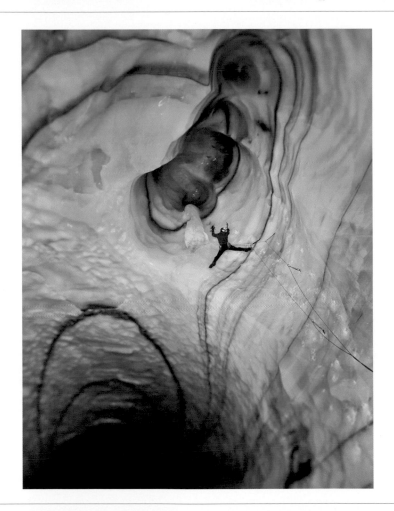

Dean Blotto Gray

Bob Allen

Gabe Rogel

Mark Newcomb on a ski expedition
near Shishapangma, Tibet

Greg Von Doersten

Corey Rich

A man strains to clip a quickdraw while rock climbing in Hell Gate Canyon, Montana

Andrew Querner

Daniel Lai

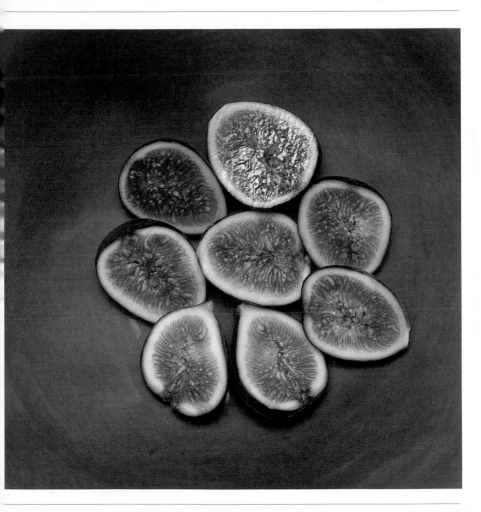

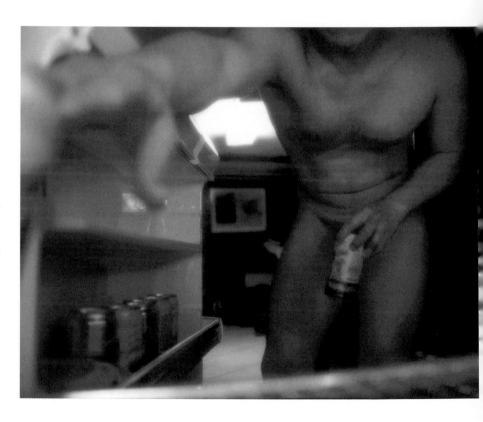

Jamie Rose

Sergio Ballivian

Jared Leeds

Robbie Shone

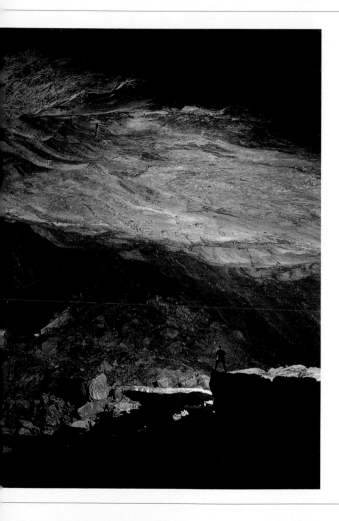

Kennan Harvey

Will Gadd clowns around on Musashi, an extreme mixed climb in Alberta, Canada

Jerry Dodrill

A skiBASE jumper does a back flip off a cliff near Lake Tahoe, California

Scott Pommier

A skateboarder jumps over a fire
hydrant on a steep San Francisco street

Greg Epperson

Eric Rorer

Mali dogon tribal woman
wearing traditional earrings

Richard Freeda

Mike Tyson

189

Robert Gallagher

Jay L. Clendenin

Ryan Donnell

Peter Dennen

Two surfers scout the break
along Higgins Beach, Maine

AURORA
PHOTOS

AURORA PHOTOS
20-36 Danforth Street, Suite 216
Portland, Maine 04101

207.828.8787
info@auroraphotos.com
http://www.auroraphotos.com

AURORA SELECT
10 East 33rd Street, Suite 1000
New York, NY 10016

646.290.7816
assignments@auroraphotos.com
http://select.auroraphotos.com/

ACKNOWLEDGEMENTS

My gratitude begins with the photographers, without whom this book would never have been possible. Thank you for making such great images, sharing your work, and contributing to Aurora Photos and this book. Along with this immense photographic talent, the staff at Aurora has brought this project to life. Collectively sharing the passion and dedication that has allowed a small company to grow, each individual has also brought their own unique aptitudes to the work. For this project, I especially thank two people: Vanessa Rodriguez, who did an immense amount of work, and Karl Schatz, who can cross between technology solutions and art. This book could not have happened without them.

Personally and professionally, my thanks and appreciation go out to everyone who has contributed to the archive.

José Azel
Portland, Maine